Proust's Overcoat

Proust's Overcoat

The True Story of One Man's Passion for All Things Proust

Lorenza Foschini

TRANSLATED FROM THE ITALIAN BY
Eric Karpeles

W11 4QR

First published in 2010 in the United States by Ecco,
an imprint of HarperCollins Publishers.

Originally published as *Il cappotto di Proust*
in Italy in 2008 by Portaparole.

The photographs on pages 5, 83, 86, 87, 118, and 121 are courtesy of Eric Karpeles. The photographs on pages xii, 6, 114, and 122 are courtesy of Marco Molendini. The photograph on page 12 is courtesy of Carlo Jansiti. All other photographs are courtesy of the author.

A CIP catalogue record is available from the British Library

9 8 7 6 5 4 3 2

ISBN 978 1 84627 271 4

www.portobellobooks.com

Designed by Suet Yee Chong
Offset by Avon DataSet Ltd, Bidford on Avon, Warwickshire

Printed and bound in the UK by
CPI Mackays, Chatham ME5 8T

To my family, a bizarre family history

Author's Note

In the process of reconstructing these events and documenting their passage, in coming to know better the people who lived them, I discovered how important even the smallest of details can be: objects of little value, furniture of questionable taste. In fact, the most common things can reveal unsuspected passions, even an old, threadbare overcoat.

Proust's Overcoat

"THE OVERCOAT WAS BEFORE ME AT LAST."

I

Beauty is always strange.

—Charles Baudelaire

I stood in that big room with the fluorescent lighting, like someone who had come to identify the body of a loved one. M. Bruson and his assistant brought out a cardboard box. They carried it delicately and with a certain detachment, as if exhuming such a meager thing were beneath them. They placed the box on a metal-topped table in the center of the room and removed its cover. All of a sudden the men, shaking out sheets of tissue paper, their arms raised, were covered in white, like two gesticulating ghosts. I was immediately overcome by the smell of camphor and mothballs.

I approached the table slowly, taking little steps, smiling with embarrassment. The overcoat was before me at last, laid out like a shroud at the bottom of the box on a large sheet of tissue paper. Stiffened by paper padding, the coat seemed to be covering something dead. Tufts of tissue were protruding from the heavily padded sleeves. I bent forward farther. It struck me that inside the box was a dummy, a plump, corpulent, barrel-chested dummy with no head or hands.

I was uncomfortable in the presence of M. Bruson. He discreetly sought not to fix his gaze upon me, but I knew that he was spying on me surreptitiously. Unable to resist, I lightly fingered the overcoat's threadbare, dark gray wool, worn smooth at the hem. It was a double-breasted coat, closed by two rows of three buttons. At some point these buttons had been moved to alter the coat for someone thinner, yet traces of where they had originally been sewn on remained visible, little buds of black thread. A small hole in the cloth suggested a missing button that must have been used to close the collar. From the black fur lapel hung a white tag, tied to a red string. I lifted it up, but there was nothing written on it. I unbuttoned the coat in hopes of finding some clue, a label indicating the name of a store or tailor: nothing.

Hopeful, I slid my hands into the pockets: again, nothing. The overcoat was lined on the inside with otter, the fur worn thin and devoured by mites. M. Bruson seemed impatient, but I wasn't quite ready to detach myself from this inert, sham figure. I decided not to leave just yet. Really, hardly several minutes had passed, and this was the overcoat Proust had wrapped about himself for years, which he spread upon himself like a blanket while in bed writing *In Search of Lost Time*. The spirit invoked in Marthe Bibesco's memoir came back to me: "At the ball, Marcel Proust sat down in front of me on a little gilded chair, as if coming out of a dream, with his fur-lined cloak, his face full of sadness, and his night-seeing eyes."

I thanked M. Bruson. Carefully, he made several small readjustments: he plumped up the paper padding, rebuttoned the coat, and buried it again under its blanket of white tissue paper. He fitted on its cardboard cover. With the help of his assistant, the box was lifted and placed back up on the highest shelf of a metal storage unit. Before leaving, I took one last look behind me. On the side of the box, in capital letters, a black felt-tip pen had been used to inscribe PROUST'S OVERCOAT. I went out, across the beautiful interior courtyard of the Musée Carnavalet, and left by the same side door through which I had entered, onto rue de Sévigné.

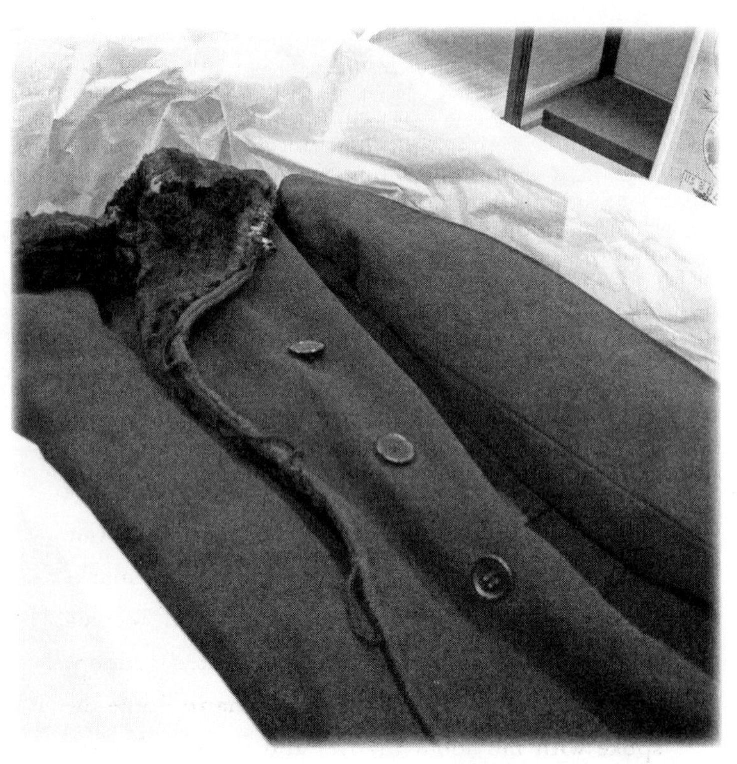

II

It all started when I interviewed Piero Tosi for a television program. Tosi is the celebrated costume designer who worked side by side on many remarkable projects with Luchino Visconti, the esteemed Italian film and theater director. That afternoon, at Tosi's house near the Piazza Navona in Rome, he spoke with me about his life and some of his extraordinary experiences. As we were finishing up, though the hour was late, I couldn't resist the temptation to ask him about Proust. I knew that in the early sixties, Tosi had been delegated by Visconti to oversee plans for shooting a film adaptation of *In*

Search of Lost Time in Paris, plans that were soon abandoned.

Tosi, though reserved, began to elaborate in great detail: "We were so enthusiastic, so hopeful about finally bringing this project to life. Luchino had already made contact with some of the biggest names in world cinema. We were talking to Laurence Olivier, Dustin Hoffman, certainly Greta Garbo, actors of international renown whose names would help finance the film. But personally, I was a bit hesitant. Lila de Nobili, a great costume designer I revere, had said to me: 'It's not possible. To make a film based on Proust is absolutely impossible. The cinema is something concrete. You can't transpose memory into film.' But Visconti was determined, and sent me to Paris to oversee the project and begin the research. I met Proust's niece, Suzy Mante-Proust, and several aristocrats who had known the models that inspired certain of the characters, such as the Duchesse de Guermantes and Baron de Charlus. I spent a lot of time speaking with them, but they had nothing I could really use. Then, one day, someone mentioned a gentleman whose name I have forgotten. . . . I know I still have his calling card somewhere, because I never threw it away. I was told that he was a collector of Proust's manuscripts and that he might be very helpful."

Tosi tracked the gentleman down, requested an appointment, and went to meet him. It wasn't a simple trip, going out and finding an office in the suburbs of Paris. Finally, Tosi arrived at sunset in front of the gates. "I remember," he told me, "a brick wall, a grove of horse chestnut trees, a factory. This gentleman was the owner of a business that manufactured perfumes. He received me in his office, a vast room with pink walls, lined with shelves laden with bars of soap. The scent of lavender and violet perfumed the air around me. As he sat behind his desk, the image I had of him was of a large nocturnal bird, black and fantastic. He spoke an old-fashioned French—marvelous, sublime."

The man sitting behind the desk proceeded to tell Tosi the extraordinary story of how a growing passion for the writings of Marcel Proust had overlapped with a serious medical condition. One summer, as a young man in Paris, he suffered what seemed to be a bout of appendicitis. An eminent surgeon was summoned to operate on the young perfume magnate. Called back to Paris from his vacation in Vichy, the doctor was Robert Proust, the brother of Marcel. Some time after the operation, the patient paid a call on his doctor, who gave him the opportunity to see some of his legendary brother's manuscript notebooks. This experience left a profound impression on the young man, and he began to hunt for anything that had to do with the great writer. He made contact with the family, with relatives, with friends. He pored over obituary listings in *Le Figaro*, and when someone who had played a part in the Proustian world died, he would attend the funeral, worming his way into the church, pretending to be a relation. Singling out the one person at the gathering who most interested him, he would ingratiate himself, initiate a conversation, then pump the person for information.

Tosi listened, rapt. At the end of this unforgettable meeting, the man revealed to Tosi that he had once possessed Marcel Proust's bedroom furniture, which he eventually donated to the great museum of the history of Paris, the Musée Carnavalet. However, he further confided, he still owned the famous overcoat, the coat in which Marcel had swaddled himself while out on various adventures and escapades, the coat that doubled as a blanket when he wrote in bed at night.

Tosi was dumbfounded. The gentleman "rose and took down from the shelves a box tied in string. He unwrapped it and pulled out a dark gray, almost black wool coat, lined in fur." Tosi described the coat to me, with his wardrobe master's all-seeing eye. "How did you happen to come to own this coat, *monsieur*?" he asked. The man recounted an astonishing tale.

It had gotten very late. I bid my farewell to Piero Tosi, fascinated and intrigued by his stories about this mysterious, obsessive collector.

Early the next morning I was awakened by a ringing telephone. It was Tosi, polite, discreet, to the point: "I found the calling card. Guérin; the fellow's name was Jacques Guérin."

JACQUES GUÉRIN.

III

At their first meeting in 1947, the writer Violette Leduc fell hopelessly in love with Jacques Guérin. Jean Genet had brought him to her small studio on rue Paul-Bert, a few steps from the Bastille, a single room whose sole window overlooked a row of trash cans. Genet entered with a tall, impeccably dressed man who had a slight tic: he would repeatedly resettle his glasses on his nose. Leduc noticed then that the man had beautifully groomed hands and that small gold buttons in the shape of chestnuts were sewn onto the cuff of his jacket sleeves. A soft mass of short black hair framed a handsome, elongated face with dreamy blue eyes. He hid his natural shyness behind extremely polite manners, which made him seem a bit aloof; he appeared to be well educated.

Apart from a few photographs, Leduc's account of Guérin provided me my first description of him. Her love for Guérin proved to be futile, given his preference for men. Yet Leduc, the author of *La Bâtarde*, recognized something of herself in Guérin—both had been children born out of wedlock. As a result of the stigma each experienced, an emptiness developed that proved impossible to fill.

Guérin was born in Paris, the son of a beautiful woman, Jeanne-Louise Guérin. In 1890, she had married Jules Giraud, an affluent wine merchant. Though very much in love with his wife, Giraud was impotent, incapable of sexual consummation. In due course, Jeanne-Louise became the mistress of her husband's close friend, Gaston Monteux, the "king" of Raoul Shoes, a wealthy Jewish man who was already married and head of a family.

In 1900 Jeanne-Louise decided to live on her own, and separated from Giraud. Although she bore two children by Monteux—Jacques in 1902, and another son, Jean, in 1903—she could not keep them with her. Social norms would not allow it. The boys grew up on the outskirts of Paris, under the watch of a nanny from the West Indies, but they saw both their mother and father on a regular basis.

According to what Guérin told writer Carlo Jansiti (his friend and my primary source for this story), his parents loved each other passionately and, even though they didn't live together, they saw each other every day. When Gaston Monteux's wife died in 1924, Guérin, a conventional son at heart, tried unsuccessfully to push his mother and father into marriage. His parents' correspondence gave testimony to an extraordinary sexual liaison; Guérin destroyed their letters when his mother died.

Jeanne-Louise Guérin, outfitted by the fashionable couturier Paul Poiret, lived in a large art-filled apartment near Parc Monceau, frequented by an artistic crowd. Erik Satie composed his song "Tendrement" for her. Gaston Monteux also loved the company of artists. A photograph shows him at his house on the Côte d'Azur, in a garden adorned with Modigliani sculptures. On one side is his son Jacques, on the other, his friend Picasso.

Jeanne-Louise was anything but conformist. After the scandal she caused at the time of her divorce, she transformed herself into a formidable businesswoman. In 1916, in association with Théophile Bader, a founder of the Galeries Lafayette department store, she took over the French perfume company known as Parfums d'Orsay, at a time when Coty and Guerlain dominated the market. But Mme Guérin was a shrewd manager and her business prospered. She soon decided to expand and moved her base of production from Neuilly to a château at Puteaux-sur-Seine, once the home of a great dandy, the Chevalier d'Orsay. On the site of this enchanting property stood a two-story building situated in a park of ancient trees. It had an imposing facade, large picture windows, and two side wings. She converted it to her factory. The grounds were charming; passing through the gates was like entering into a strange garden where intoxicating perfumes came not from the flowers or vegetation but rather from the open doors and windows of the building, which exuded the scents of jasmine, rose, and violet.

As a young man, Guérin was sent to Toulouse to

study chemistry. On his return, he worked alongside his mother at the helm of the company, learning trade secrets for a business that would soon become exclusively his. All told, Guérin would devote more than sixty years of his life to Parfums d'Orsay.

By the 1920s Jeanne-Louise was acknowledged as a highly successful entrepreneur and a captain of industry. Parfums d'Orsay then employed about five hundred people. The business included a printing house and a package design studio as well as manufacturing and shipping offices. A large, bright room housed women who worked sorting through white, yellow, orange, and crimson rose petals, which, once picked over, were piled high in huge wicker baskets. There was a small inner room, a sanctum sanctorum that housed the perfumery's "organ," an imposing semicircular display unit lined with flasks of essences the researchers used from time to time in their work. In the laboratory, the heart of the operation, workmen and chemists in white smocks watched over sixty-five gleaming metal cylinders in which the essences of scents were conserved. Once verified and analyzed, the essences were blended according to a secret formula, about which any one person knew only one part. They were then decanted into a suspension of alcohol and expressly distilled just for the length of time required to obtain the perfect homogeneity for the company's signature perfumes.

Those chemists who had the good fortune over long years of practice to develop that special olfactory gift for memorizing scents and scent combinations were known as "noses." Like a musician practicing scales all day long, a "nose" worked until he was capable of recognizing and combining some three thousand different fragrances in order to achieve perfect harmony. Presented with a scent for his consideration, a "nose" could determine what was lacking in the fragrance, that necessary *je ne sais quoi* required to heighten its personality. It could take many long days and nights before that moment arrived, but when it did, the awareness of what element was needed seemed to emerge naturally, crowning a labor of many months. Knowledge of the laws of chemistry alone was insufficient to the task of predicting the possible reactions and mutations of certain essences on certain bodies. In order to assemble a blend worthy of the name "perfume," a "nose" had to cultivate an unfailing exactitude for the essential combination of fragrances to master the true science of scents.

Under the reign of Mme Guérin, perfumes were created that would become known around the world: La Finette, L'Ambrée, L'Aveu, Le Charme d'Orsay, Le Chevalier à la Rose, and above all Le Dandy. This perfume perfectly represented both the taste of the period and Jeanne-Louise's refined style. In 1916, she commissioned an opaque black crystal perfume bottle specifically for Le Dandy, with octagonal facets, a large pearl stopper, and a gilded label. The bottle was designed by Louis Suë and André Mare, architects who, at the same period, also created the designs for the Parfums d'Orsay stores on rue de la Paix in Paris and Fifth Avenue in New York. The Paris boutique, with its imposing facade, was situated on a corner with a modest front and a covered entrance that contrasted with the imposing shop windows—two on rue de la Paix, five others along rue Daunou. In pure Art Deco style, the veined-marble window surrounds were decorated with flowering branches, garlands of fruits, and bronze drapery. Inside, the fantasy scenes of Suë and Mare were given equal freedom.

By 1936, Jeanne-Louise had bought out all her investors, and soon after, her son took over as director. The firm went through a time of crisis, but Jacques Guérin skillfully stabilized the situation. Though he remained head of the firm for over fifty years, and lived to almost one hundred, Guérin retained few memories of his business career; that work was never the primary focus of his life. His real passion lay in his growing collection of rare books, precious manuscripts, and artists' papers. His success as a collector, however, was undoubtedly enhanced by business savvy, honed from a long professional life. Guérin's gift for unearthing and safeguarding one-of-a-kind treasures had much in common with his flair for identifying enticing and commercially viable fragrances.

Though he refused to think of himself as a bibliophile, by the time he was in his twenties he was already known as one. In 1923, Erik Satie inscribed a note "To my good friend Jacques Guérin, the charming bibliophile." Proust captured the animating consciousness behind Guérin's love of books:

"... that which enables us to see through the bodies of poets and lets us look into their souls is not their eyes, nor the events of their lives, but their books, precisely where their souls, with an instinctive desire, would like to be immortalized."

Guérin had made his first purchase when he was eighteen, a rare first edition of Guillaume Apollinaire's early short-story collection *L'Hérésiarque et Cie*. At the time, Apollinaire was practically unknown, and Guérin bought the book for a song, at thirteen francs. As an old man he recalled with pride this first transaction, aware that the book would have cost him millions of francs had he sought to acquire it years later. For an industrialist's son—why deny it?—this elicited an incalculable pleasure. He also owned a drawing of Apollinaire as wounded soldier on the front during the First World War, that was made by Picasso. Guérin had come across the portrait on a visit to Picasso in his studio. Picasso had never been a favorite painter of Guérin's, but Guérin admired the Spaniard's extraordinary gift for self-promotion. The drawing of Apollinaire didn't strike him as especially beautiful, but he praised it out of politeness. Picasso

detached the portrait from his sketchbook and inscribed it, "To Jacques."

Guérin also had a taste for secrets and a love for hidden things. During the long hours at the factory, Guérin labored alongside his employees, surrounded by thousands of little vials of fragrance. His day's work behind him, he would often head back to the center of Paris in a pale green 1929 Buick convertible. Parking his car near the Parfums d'Orsay store, he would begin his circuit on rue de la Paix. He loved to stroll in and out of the city's antiquarian bookstores, scanning the shelves for any new inventory, sniffing out finds with his "nose" for the unique. As recounted by Guérin to Jansiti (for an article in *Le Figaro Littéraire* published in the 1980s), he was making the usual rounds one day in 1935 and came into the rue du Faubourg Saint-Honoré. He saw a bookshop he had never noticed before, just across from Hermès. He went into the shop and began to browse. The owner approached him, asking if he could be of help, if there were any writers in particular who interested him.

Guérin demurred, but mentioned Baudelaire and Proust.

The bookseller, named Lefebvre, made a gesture of surprise. Only a few minutes earlier he had bought some proofs corrected in the hand of Marcel Proust. The seller had just left. In addition to autograph manuscripts, Lefebvre had also been informed that Proust's desk and bookcase were for sale, but he had declined these, as he was not set up to deal with furniture. The bookseller said that the man would soon be returning to the store to pick up a check.

Of all his favorite writers, Guérin was most fascinated by Proust. He had begun to read him at the age of twenty and had never stopped. He was twenty-seven during the summer of 1929 when his life intersected with the writer's family. Dr. Robert Proust, Marcel's brother, was called to Guérin's bedside after what seemed to be an appendicitis attack and made the decision to operate. The patient was sent to a hospital on rue Boileau.

As was the fashion in those days, several weeks after his recovery the young man presented himself at the doctor's office to offer his thanks and pay his bill. He rang the bell at the building on avenue Hoche and was let into a large apartment, the home

DR. ROBERT PROUST.

befitting a surgeon of some reputation, luxuriously decorated in the questionable bourgeois taste of the period. Guérin recoiled slightly as he took it all in—the overstuffed sofas with their slightly concave backs, the tapestries depicting bucolic scenes, the incredibly textured paintings on the walls, impressive even to someone accustomed to the canvases of Soutine and Courbet in his own home. In keeping with the late-nineteenth-century taste for heavy furnishings, nothing in the doctor's office was not somber or depressing.

Guérin was transfixed by the massiveness of the furniture, including a three-sectioned black bookcase and an imposing desk with brass-inlaid drawers. The doctor mistook his patient's scrutiny for admiration. He explained to Guérin that the pieces of furniture had once belonged to his brother, Marcel, who had inherited them from their father, Dr. Adrien Proust. Marcel had valued them highly, and now Robert cherished them as mementos of his late brother and father.

The young man's fascination with his doctor's brother was palpable. Graciously, Robert opened one of the glass doors of the formidable bookcase.

He pointed to the tall stacks of manuscript notebooks. Arranged in no particular order, these were the complete works of Marcel Proust, written in his own hand. Guérin's eyes opened wide. The doctor removed one notebook from the stacks and handed it to him. The young man opened it and found inside an arabesque of words, scratched-out sentences, insertions, notes, marginal annotations; a cathedral of vowels, consonants, uppercase letters, lowercase letters, erasures, and changes, which Guérin scrutinized hungrily. He strained to decipher the irregular, brittle, jerky handwriting that filled every available space, page after page. Proust's downward-slanting script was exceedingly angular, entangled, hastily scrawled. As described by his housekeeper Céleste, Proust would write in bed, a notebook in one hand stretched in the air, his pen in the other hand. Pages would scatter upon the bed and fall on the rug. Céleste would tenderly gather them up with loving care and attention.

At the time of Guérin's formal post-operative visit with Robert Proust, Marcel Proust had been dead only seven years. In that space of time, his life and death had already attained legendary status.

Guérin had heard much about the writer's eccentric life: his cork-lined room on boulevard Haussmann, the intense cold in his bedroom on rue Hamelin, where the central heating was turned off to avoid aggravating his asthmatic condition, the nightly vigils to bring his great work to completion in an incessant race against death. He was engaged in an ongoing struggle against an illness for which he refused either medication or proper care. As Proust described it, death was a stranger who had chosen to take up residence in his brain, coming and going; "a too considerate tenant," was how he put it. "I was surprised to see that she was not beautiful," he wrote in a preface to *Tender Stocks*, his friend Paul Morand's book. "I had always imagined that death was." In a moment when this "too considerate tenant" was absent, Proust finally succeeded in bringing his great work to completion, inscribing the word *fin* in the determined, assured strokes Guérin now saw emblazoned before him on the yellowed pages of a worn notebook.

Proust had awoken one day in the spring of 1922—at four o'clock in the afternoon—and said to his housekeeper, "Something wonderful happened last night, Céleste." Usually when he awoke, he would remain silent, but that afternoon he looked up at her and announced:"My dear Céleste, I have to tell you about it, it's great news. Last night, I wrote the word *fin*. Now I can die."

"Oh, *Monsieur*, don't speak like that. I can see that you are very happy. I, too, am so happy that you've finally succeeded in finishing what you set out to do. But I know you well enough, and I'm afraid that you aren't really finished yet. All these little pieces of paper still need assembling; you still have all the corrections to oversee."

"That is something else, Céleste. The important thing is that I'm no longer worried now. I haven't given my life for nothing."

Writing *In Search of Lost Time* had given meaning to his life. Proust loved to repeat the words of St. John, so much appreciated by Ruskin: "Work while you still have the light."

Guérin, who regularly socialized with artists and writers, had amassed a considerable collection of anecdotes and details about the last months of the novelist's life, when Proust was engaged in a battle against time and against death. Now, seated in the oppressive office of Proust's brother, he understood the full impact of this word *fin*, written with such clarity and force, detached from the body of the text. He was envious of the doctor for possessing anything so precious, something at once so intimate and at the same time so universal. The envy that drove Guérin as a collector, his intense longing for direct contact with the ineffable, spurred him to try to extract some further memory from Robert Proust, to get the doctor to reveal some intimacy he had the privilege of sharing with his genius of a brother.

Guérin told him it would mean a great deal to see the first edition of *Swann's Way*, which Proust had had to pay Bernard Grasset to print for him after every other publisher rejected it. Of course he would have made his brother a gift of this. The doctor looked at him, taken aback, unable to make sense of the request. He had just offered this young man the honor of holding in his hands Marcel's own handwritten notebook, certainly an unforgettable opportunity. Now he asked to see an old printed edition? Robert Proust told him he was sorry, but he had no such book. This response, offered rather brusquely, troubled Guérin. He thanked the doctor and took his leave. Coming away from avenue Hoche, he kept ruminating, somewhat surprised, on the doctor's last words, wondering, with his irrepressible curiosity, what might have really been the nature of the relationship between the two brothers.

Such were the memories that came flooding back to Guérin as he waited in the bookstore in the Faubourg Saint-Honoré early one evening in 1935. Several weeks earlier, on the twenty-second of May, the death of Robert Proust had been reported. Now, in one of those strange twists of fate, Guérin found himself awaiting someone who might provide him access to Proust's intimate circle, a world to which he was still incredibly drawn.

The sound of the bookshop's bell roused him. The door opened abruptly and an insolent young man came in, his hat tilted to one side. Guérin carefully gave him a once-over, from head to toe. He was amused—no one could possibly have seemed more out of his element here than this cocky youth among these fusty stacks of old books. Still, Guérin found something quite appealing about him, a seductive mixture of allure and impudence that reminded him of the handsome young men he found in Montmartre and Pigalle.

The bookseller introduced them: Monsieur Guérin, Monsieur Werner.

Guérin looked him over again with a certain disdain, then questioned him as to how he came to have Proust's furniture to sell, clearly suspicious of the means by which this fellow came into possession of such things.

Werner told him that Dr. Proust had inherited Marcel's furniture when his brother died. When the doctor died a few weeks ago, his wife had made the decision to vacate her apartment immediately. Their daughter, Suzy, removed the majority of furniture and other effects that once belonged to her uncle Marcel, but she left behind his desk and his bookcase. No one wanted them. Werner offered them to Guérin for 1,500 francs.

Usually a very shrewd negotiator, Guérin accepted the terms immediately, without a moment's hesitation. He would always wonder about that. At that same instant, Werner must have understood both Guérin's hunger and his financial ability to satisfy that hunger handsomely. He had felt Guérin size him up, but now Werner knew that he was the one in control. He had something the other desperately wanted: from the start, the relationship was tinged with a kind of sadism.

Werner was insistent that everything be removed immediately. The apartment would be completely cleared out in a matter of hours and whatever was not spoken for he would haul off to a showroom of Drouot's, the auctioneers, that would take any kind of merchandise that came in.

For the second time in his life, Guérin found himself making his way to the house of Robert Proust, this time with a flippant salesman sitting casually beside him in the Buick. As he drove, he thought about his first meeting with Marthe Dubois-Amiot, Robert's wife, now his widow—the woman who was in such a hurry to get rid of the furniture he had just bought from Werner. They had been introduced once at a formal celebration in honor of her husband, an event coincidentally hosted by a member of Guérin's extended family. That occasion also marked the last time he saw the illustrious doctor. The dinner had taken place just a few months after Guérin's first visit to Robert's apartment on avenue Hoche.

From 1921 to 1926, Robert Proust had been director of the Tenon Hospital, one of the premier radiotherapy centers in Paris, specializing in tumor research. By the time of this testimonial dinner in 1929, he was the head of a private cancer research foundation. At fifty-six, a goodly age for the period, he was an imposing man, tall and solid. His face resembled his brother's, but was rounder; his sad eyes were less magnetic; his mustache was less fastidious. He always appeared to be shouldering a weight, and this made him seem heavier than he really was.

When his brother died in 1922, Robert Proust had inherited, along with most everything else, all the manuscripts that were found in Marcel's last apartment on rue Hamelin. The doctor's responsibilities as staff oncologist and chief surgeon at one of Paris's largest hospitals absorbed him completely, yet from the day of his brother's death he had also assigned himself the extremely difficult and highly technical task of preparing the last volumes of *In Search of Lost Time* for posthumous publication. In this endeavor, he had to work in close collaboration with an editorial team from Marcel's publishers, La Nouvelle Revue Française, under the direction of Jacques Rivière. In addition to having been a trusted friend, Rivière was also professionally bound to Proust in a working relationship that endured through to the writer's last days. Rivière had overseen the publication of the first volumes of the novel and Marcel had charged him to publish his complete notebooks "in case of disagreeable events."

But the notebooks remained the property of Robert Proust, who retained the publication rights. At first, the collaboration was courteous, nearly affectionate, but the honeymoon was short-lived. The doctor's complex personality made any straightforward communication nearly impossible. He could be fierce or easily offended, prudent or extremely arrogant. Mostly he was steadfast about the correctness of his own judgment. The final three volumes of *In Search of Lost Time* not published in Marcel Proust's lifetime—*The Captive, The Fugitive, Time Regained*—were edited under the iron will of Robert Proust, who silently and inexorably attempted to impose an absence of any discrepancies in the unpublished texts.

In vain, Rivière and co-editor Gaston Gallimard repeatedly requested to inspect the written manuscripts. In 1926, four years after Marcel Proust's death, Robert Proust was still the only person alive who knew what happened in *Time Regained*. Consumed with monklike devotion, the doctor continued to block publication of the last volumes for months. He steadfastly refused to yield either to Rivière's respectfulness or his authority. Day after day, relations grew increasingly strained. Exasperated by the doctor's dilatory methods, irritated at having to work through him as an intermediary, exhausted, and maybe already terminally ill, Rivière finally delegated the responsibility of revision to his collaborators. Gallimard took over, but as late as the summer of 1931, he was still writing to Robert Proust in exasperation, "I must remind you that a definitive edition of the complete novel has been held up for long enough, awaiting your decision regarding the text of *The Fugitive*." The editors working on the text, Jean Paulhan and Benjamin Crémieux, added their voices: "We ask you earnestly to permit us to work, under your control, from the original manuscript." The doctor maintained his dominance, in a position of increasing solitude. He made a decision to discard the typed manuscript that existed for *The Fugitive*, pages Marcel had dictated to a secretary when he was too weak to write, which, according to Robert, disrupted the continuity of the last books. If the editors insisted on retaining the typed manuscript pages, it would jeopardize publication of a definitive text.

Was it finding himself so far out of his element, all the while being absolutely unwilling to abdicate control, that gave Robert the skittish expression he maintained until he died? His reticent and evasive manner contrasted sharply with that of his younger brother, who, even though seriously ill, had managed to the end to maintain a lightness, an elegance, and also the sense of irony of a young man destined not to know old age.

At the testimonial dinner in honor of the renowned oncologist, no one was aware of Robert Proust's "other job." Across the table, Guérin had a chance to study the doctor and his wife, Marthe.

No one would have mistaken them for a happily married couple. Robert was quite corpulent and had a melancholic, repressed air. Marthe, dressed in black, was very thin, emaciated. Though she was withdrawn and obviously in a dreadful state, Guérin approached her as soon as the meal was over, eagerly on the trail of new stories and revelations, much too determined to be deterred from unearthing further secrets of the Proust family legacy. Marthe had gotten up and gone to sit in front of the fire, upright and severe. Guérin followed and sat himself on a low stool at her feet.

Deferentially, he whispered to her about the privilege bestowed upon him by her husband when, after an office consultation, the doctor had allowed his patient to gaze upon some of his brother's notebooks.

The woman listened, a smile frozen on her face, and made no reply. He carried on speaking about the manuscripts, letters, and papers the doctor and she had inherited and the fascination they must provide.

Mme Proust had an almost strident, nasal voice, and it rose above the din in the room to insist he not speak to her of such things. She and her husband were mired in a sea of papers. There was an unbelievable quantity. But they were certainly going to deal with those masses of notebooks and endless piles of letters. They would put fire to everything. They would burn them all.

She regained her calm demeanor, and then smiled broadly at him. She seemed rather pleased with herself.

Guérin was stunned by this reply. He watched the flames darting out of the fireplace beside him. Flames such as these, he thought, would be trained on the earthly remains of a genius. He got up and left the room, dazed and incredulous, inconsolable, thinking that one didn't need war or revolution for there to be destruction. Families take it as their right to reduce to ashes any precious vestiges they choose.

Marthe Dubois-Amiot, whose family came from Aix-les-Bains, wasn't always so bitter and irritable. When she had come into the Proust family as a bride in 1903, she was a gracious young woman, and like most young women of that time, somewhat naive; enthusiastically, she entered into the ar-

DR. ADRIEN PROUST.

ranged marriage. This act of joining together two families had been prompted by Robert Proust's father, Dr. Adrien Proust, who was a frequent visitor at her house on rue de Messine. He and Marthe's mother were known to be close friends: in fact, they were lovers. Marthe had known Dr. Proust as a friend of the family who regularly came and went from the house; she was quite content to be engaged to his son. After all, Robert was a promising young man who had chosen a medical career like his father. Having scrupulously prepared a doctoral thesis on female genital surgery, he pursued his research on hermaphroditism.

But if Marthe remained ignorant of the circumstances that had led to her engagement, Mme Proust and her sons must certainly have harbored some suspicions. A decidedly ill humor hovered over the wedding preparations, which, according to Marcel, were organized as secretly as possible. Even the bride-to-be's brother was kept in the dark.

For a while, the wedding preparations turned Proust's daily habits upside down. Twice he had to get up far earlier than usual, first to make the acquaintance of the young girl, then for the en-

MME ADRIEN PROUST.

gagement dinner, held on January 24 in the Proust family's rue de Courcelles apartment. Furthermore, he was under the pressure of a deadline, needing to submit the completed manuscript of his translation of Ruskin's *Bible d'Amiens* before March 1, and there was still a great deal of work left to do on it. "This wedding couldn't have happened at a worse time," he moaned.

Nevertheless, at noon on February 2, 1903, Proust, exhausted, arrived at the Church of St. Augustin to act as witness and stand up as his brother's best man. He hadn't slept for three nights and his appearance was frightful. He was dressed astoundingly, swaddled in multiple layers of clothing; he wore three sweaters underneath a jacket, and three coats on top of that. He had wrapped his chest and neck in flannel, bits of which poked out from the collar of his shirt. According to his young cousin Valentine Thomson, Proust looked like Lazarus resurrected from the dead, "like someone in a cocoon made of black wool. Feeling it was necessary to excuse his appearance as he passed each row, he intoned in a deep voice that he couldn't have dressed himself otherwise, that he had been sick for months, that he would be even sicker later that night, and that none of it was his fault."

Yet Mme Proust surpassed even her eccentric son. Due to an attack of rheumatism, she arrived at the ceremony in an ambulance. (How often it happens that our minor maladies betray our far more serious conditions.) She was unable to attend the reception afterward at the house on rue de Messine. Proust did attend, but once there, he managed to collapse in exhaustion. "Robert's wedding quite literally killed me," he later wrote to Mme Catusse, a friend of his mother's. He kept to his bed for two weeks.

From the Faubourg Saint-Honoré, with the young M. Werner in tow, it was a quick trip to Robert Proust's home and office. It was as if, six years later, fate was leading him to a place where he had never expected to find himself again. Once admitted to the ground-floor apartment, he saw that everything had been removed. He felt the air of sadness that lingers after forced departures. What had once been a residence of long standing was now completely abandoned; wallpaper was stripped from the walls, a layer of dirt covered the oak parquet floors. In the entryway, stacks of books were piled up to the ceiling. Guérin made his way into the rooms that had once been decorated in that bourgeois taste he had found so dispiriting on his first visit. Now he found the rooms empty and desolate. Coming into what had been the office where he had once breathlessly fingered Marcel Proust's manuscript notebooks, he noticed, solitary and poignant, the two massive pieces of furniture that had belonged to the writer. He recognized the huge, clumsy, tarnished black pear-wood desk in the style of the second empire, with its aristocratic pretensions. Two columns of drawers decorated with double lines of brass inlay flanked the legroom; three more gilded drawers were fitted out with brass handles, spread across the desktop. Next to the desk stood the bookcase from which Robert Proust had removed a notebook to show Guérin. The inside was now piteously empty, stripped even of the shelves that used to display the books Proust held most dear to him.

A funereal mood hung over this atmosphere of disarray. The apartment was plundered, devastated.

Guérin felt he was bearing witness to the end of an era. Strangely, the furniture seemed to be appealing to him for help. In *Swann's Way* the Narrator explains

> *the Celtic belief that the souls of those we have lost are held captive in some lesser being, in an animal, a vegetable, an inanimate object, in effect lost to us until the day, which for some of us never comes, when we find ourselves walking near a tree and it dawns on us that this object is their prison. The souls shudder, they call out to us; and as soon as we have heard them, the spell is broken. Liberated by us, they triumph over death, and come to live among us once again.*

Guérin asked Werner, who was just going out to arrange transport for his purchases, about the books stacked up in the entryway. The young man told him that they were books that had belonged to Marcel Proust. Mme Proust, the doctor's wife, had systematically ripped out whatever dedications in them she could find because she hadn't wanted Marcel's name to endure.

At that moment Guérin had the impression of being somehow singled out to make amends, to intervene in an act of salvation, to make reparations for injustices committed. He experienced this powerfully, as an obligation, one he could not ignore.

Werner went out on his errand. Left alone, Guérin paced through the many rooms of the apartment. On a mantelpiece, two books caught his eye: *Blue Hydrangeas* and *The Bats*, both by Robert de Montesquiou. One after the other he opened them. Each held an incredibly long, adulatory message from its author to Marcel Proust. Guérin now knew these inscriptions were fugitives, having escaped the devastating fury of Mme Robert Proust.

When Werner returned with help, the desk and bookcase were packed and moved out. Returning once more to his car, again with Werner beside him, Guérin drove toward his own house, followed behind by the moving van. Thinking back over the course of a long, strange day, he must have wondered about the chain of events that led him here, driving home with this improbable young man at his side.

The faculty of reason is incapable of helping us understand why we do what we do. "Our intelligence is not the most subtle of instruments, the strongest, or the most appropriate for grasping the truth," Proust wrote in *The Fugitive*, and that

> *is only one more reason to start with the intelligence and not with unconscious intuitions or a predetermined faith in presentiment. It is only very slowly, case by case, that life allows us to realize what is most important to our hearts, to our spirits, and that we do not learn by reasoning but by other powers. The intelligence itself ultimately acknowledges the superiority of these powers and abdicates reasoning to them, accepting its role as collaborator and servant.*

Guérin drove to the quiet corner of Paris where he lived. Rue Berton was situated in a secluded, bucolic spot, where occasional vestiges of countryside still remained. His was the only house on the block. An old tarred roadway led beyond his house to what once had been Balzac's house, then branched off into a vast park, the Eaux de Passy, where, long ago, Marie Antoinette had come to bathe. In the years to come, this charming enclave would succumb to much development. The road leading there would one day be named avenue

Marcel Proust, but that happened much later, beyond the realm of even Guérin's imagination.

The van was unloaded. His new acquisitions safely in the house, Guérin invited Werner to sit with him by the fire. The day had been highly emotional, but still he felt unsatisfied, unfulfilled. He wanted to know more about this abandoned furniture. Guérin was especially anxious to learn about the fate of the manuscripts and notebooks Robert Proust had shown him that once filled the bookcase. Intuitively, from the moment Guérin had seen them, he had divined the importance of the manuscripts, had understood them to be infinitely precious. He was unprepared for what Werner had to tell him.

Learning of this interest in Marcel Proust, Werner expressed frustration, regretted their not having met just a week earlier. In the previous eight days, the contents of Mme Proust's apartment had been packed up and moved out, and in the process mountains of paper were taken out into the courtyard on avenue Hoche and burned. Perhaps unconscious of the cruel pain he was inflicting,

Werner began to enumerate methodically what had been destroyed: masses of paper covered in writing; lengthy, cobbled-together "paperoles," bound folios of notes that were ripped apart; notebooks; letters, more letters, innumerable letters. There had been too much paper for them to burn it all.

In an increasingly anguished state, Guérin interrupted him to ask what had become of the notebooks written in Marcel's hand once shown to him by the doctor. Werner told him that Mme Proust had instructed him to save those because of the doctor's personal attachment to them. They had been carefully stashed away. A publisher had alerted their daughter Suzy to the possibility that these papers might be worth a fortune, so she had taken them and locked them away in a safe. When Marthe heard about their potential value, she stopped the burning. All the books and papers left behind had been offered to Lefebvre, who bought them all, and then Guérin had purchased everything from him.

So that's that, thought Guérin, as he listened to Werner. Treasures were spared from Marthe's destructive folly only when she became remorseful at having destroyed things that might have been lucrative. But the feeling that had seized Guérin back in the doctor's apartment was rekindled in him now, a confused but determined need to try and remedy what devastation had been wrought. Guérin had no way of knowing exactly what had been burned and what might have been spared. It would take him many years of desperate searching before he could rest, confident he had done everything possible to preserve what remained of Proust's earthly possessions.

Hoping that some more material might yet be salvaged, Guérin urged Werner to undertake a thorough search of everything he had carted away. He asked him to report back about whatever he might find; surely there were some "paperoles" still left unburned. He instructed Werner to tell Marthe that she could set any price she wanted. He showed Werner out and took himself off to bed.

The following evening, after having moved everything out of the avenue Hoche apartment, Werner found his way back to the house on rue Berton. The young secondhand goods dealer came in holding an old hatbox that had come from Lewis, the celebrated turn-of-the-century fashion boutique on rue Royale, its yellow label still pasted on. Werner was barely acknowledged by Guérin, who grabbed the box out of his hands, desperate to see what it held. Rifling through the hastily gathered papers stuffed inside, Guérin was able to make a connoisseur's quick, knowing assessment: letters, drawings, photographs, three or four books. As determinedly as he had opened the box he closed it up again. He counted out three thousand francs, handed them to Werner, and dismissed him.

Once alone, Guérin reopened what he must have looked upon as a treasure chest. Night was falling and there was scant daylight coming in through the room's large windows. Under the light of a lamp, he pulled from the hatbox letters Proust had once received, as well as letters he had written but never posted. With intense regard, Guérin glanced at delicate sheets of white, ivory, and turquoise paper and then at several heavier Bristol sheets embossed with insignias or interlaced initials. He recognized the signatures of Jean Cocteau, André Gide, Robert de Montesquiou, Sidney Schiff, Reynaldo Hahn, Anna de Noailles. Randomly, he picked out a letter and began to read: "Dear Jean, When death had more of a hold on me, a year or so ago, I could neither read nor write a letter. However, I did make an exception. . . ."

Guérin didn't finish; he let the unmailed letter to Jean Cocteau drop out of his hands and immediately began to read another. He read some lines, then dropped it, and then another, and another, until there were no more letters. He reached back into the hatbox again and extracted an unruly mass of papers made up of individual tiny sheets that separated and fluttered down to the floor. Picking some up, he discovered that these were notes Proust had scrawled to Céleste in his last days, when he no longer had the power to speak. "Why did I hear the bell ring in here?" one read, a handful of words tremulously dashed off in a handwriting that had become fragile, unsteady and fleeting. Looking upon these few jerky strokes of the pen, Guérin keenly felt the presence of Proust caught in the state of feverish solitude and reverberating silence that enshrouded him in his last days.

He reached back in and pulled out some scribbled pen drawings. One was a sketch of a man seated at a piano on which lay the score from Reynaldo

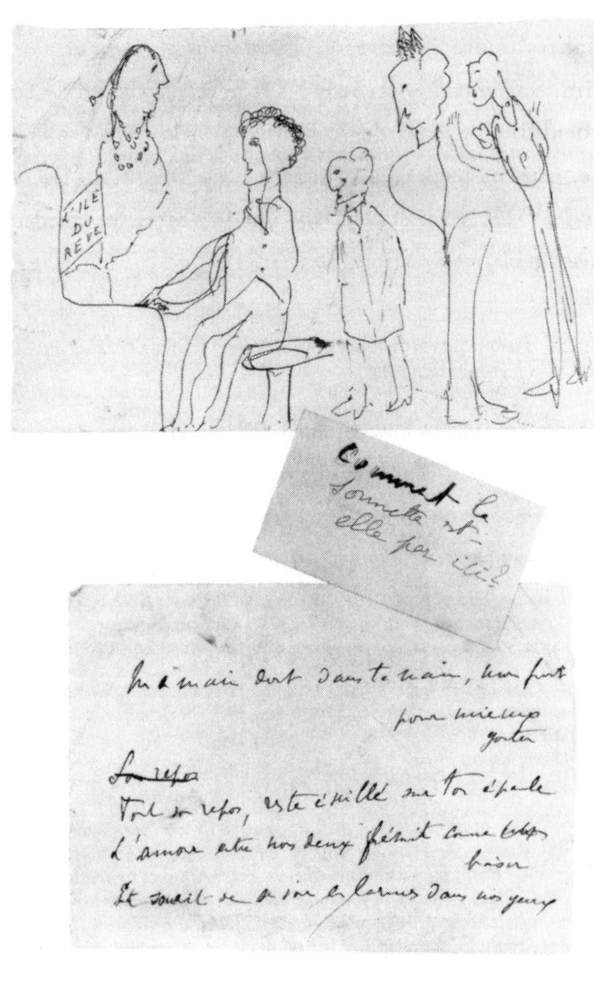
L'ILE DU REVE
Comment la sonnette est-elle par ici?
pour mieux goûter
L'amour entre nos deux frémit comme un baiser

Hahn's opera *L'Ile du rêve*. Two women stood beside him, one with a matronly air, the other sullen, with a beaklike nose, and two formal gentlemen in black tie. On the back of a program for a recital of Gounod's *Faust*, Proust had sketched a man wearing a straw hat, below which he wrote:

> I am a sailor, my song is a round
> Comme ci, comme ça
> And I know how to charm the brunette
> and the blonde
> Couçi couça.

This was followed by a love poem:

> My hand sleeps in your hand, my
> forehead, to better savor
> All repose, rests wide awake on your
> shoulder.
> The love between us two trembles like a
> kiss
> And smiles to see tears in our eyes.

REYNALDO HAHN.

Guérin reached into the bottom of the hatbox and pulled out several photographs, most of them yellowed with age. One showed an elegantly dressed young man in a derby hat, a cane in his hand and a gold watch chain slung from one pocket to another across his vest. At the bottom, the inscription read, "To Marcel, Reynaldo." (Was the love poem Guérin had just read meant for Reynaldo Hahn, Proust's lover and intimate friend?) On the back of the photo he read "Paris, Otto, 3 place de la Madeleine." Otto was the photographer in *The Captive* whose study of Odette, posed as if she were royalty, Swann had found pretentious.

Another photograph showed Marcel and Robert Proust as very young boys in matching dresses with piqué collars. They wore small wax-buttoned, polished boots with white Scottish wool socks, and double-breasted jackets with beautiful silk tassel ties. Was Robert's arm gripping his brother's sleeve to suggest protection and support? Or was it the contrary, that Robert was clinging to Marcel, in need of his older brother's greater authority? Another photo showed the brothers even younger, in baby gowns delicately decorated with lacework collars and

wrists. Robert's curly head lay on his brother's shoulder as Marcel grasped his younger brother's waist in one hand and clutched his chubby little hand in the other. A double portrait, taken during the first years of their adolescence, revealed that while the faces of the brothers had certain physical features in common, their expressions were entirely dissimilar. As little men in a photograph taken at the studio of Hermann and Company, the adolescent brothers were posed in a conventional late-nineteenth-century setup. (It was a time when fashionable taste skated perilously close to kitsch.) Perched on a railing behind a small-tiered fountain, Marcel gazed at his younger brother with a slightly ironic smile—was it the comedy of the situation that inspired his expression? Robert, seated across from him, his hat resting on his knees, was unsmiling and seemed rather put out, avoiding the arm his brother slid along the railing toward him. Slightly perplexed, caught off guard, Robert seemed to be in a very serious mood as compared to his brother. Why was he so gloomy? Was the distance he seemed intent on maintaining motivated by fear of getting his boots wet from the fountain, or was it more a question of

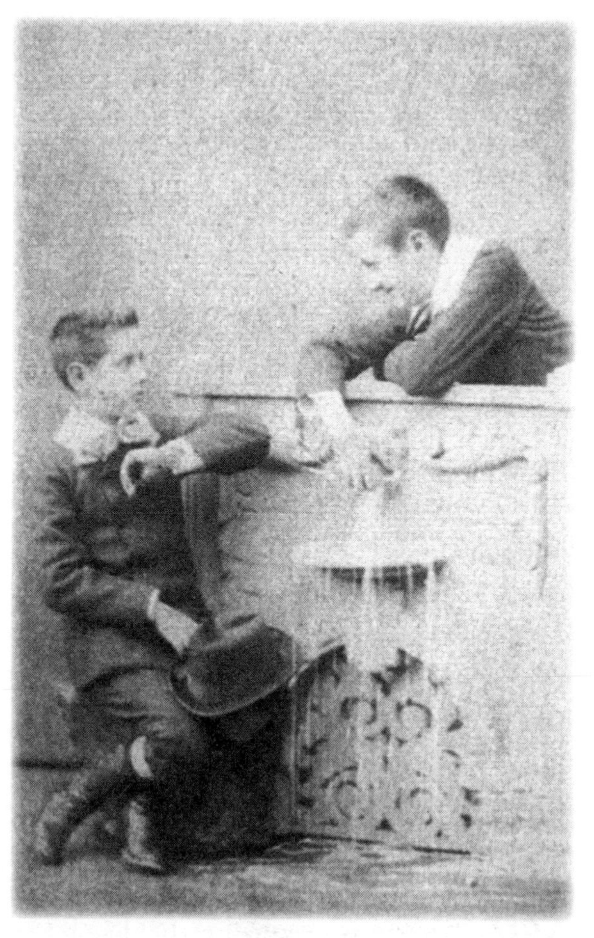

autonomy, of distance from his brother? Scrutinizing the image, Guérin sought to divine the underlying nature of their relationship. How many words did the brothers speak to each other; how many did they not speak?

The photo was dated 1883. Twelve at the time, Proust had been attending the Lycée Condorcet for a year, along with his friend from elementary school, Jacques Bizet, son of Georges Bizet, the composer of *Carmen*. Though the two boys were bound in deep friendship, these feelings would soon intensify for Proust, erupting into infatuation. Proust's mother was alerted to the situation and was sufficiently worried to forbid her son from going out with his friend. Who could have informed her of what was going on between the two boys? Who set off the alarm in her?

In the correspondence between Bizet and Proust, published long afterward, several letters help illuminate this development and how it played out within the Proust family. Five years after the photo was taken, looking back at their earlier bond, a now seventeen-year-old Proust, still smitten, wrote teasingly to Bizet in June 1888 about what or who might have tipped off his mother when they were twelve:

> *Maybe it was your appearance, or more likely she heard my brother talking about you, coming into the room when he could have been saying something malicious about you to Baignères, because you and I often did misbehave together, but it was especially because of me and my excessive affection for you. Maybe my brother . . .*

Robert was the principal suspect for having exposed their deepening connection. It is quite possible that Robert may have spoken out about his older brother's behavior in good faith, and not out of spite. So unlike Marcel, Robert was athletic, passionate about math, a reluctant reader, an exemplary son.

Certainly the Proust family was beginning to understand Marcel's inclinations, but as was true in all bourgeois households at the time, no one spoke of it. What one knew, one never discussed. All the same, one knew.

In *The Captive,* Proust wrote:

In certain untruthful families, a brother who has come to call without any apparent reason and makes some casual inquiry on the doorstep as he leaves, appearing scarcely to listen to the response, indicates to his brother that this inquiry was the sole object of his visit, for the brother is quite familiar with that air of detachment, those words uttered as though in parentheses and at the last moment, having himself had frequent recourse to use them himself. Similarly, there are pathological families, kindred spirits, fraternal temperaments, initiated into that mute language which enables the members of a family to understand each other without speaking.

These words remind me of what Jean Chalon, writer and, for decades, literary critic for *Le Figaro*, told me when I met him in Paris. "In the summer of 1982 I met a very old man, a M. de Chantenesse. His father had been a doctor, a friend of Dr. Adrien Proust's; their families lived near one another on boulevard Malesherbes. Dr. Chantenesse and Dr. Proust used to love chatting together and going for strolls around the neighborhood. One day, Dr. Chantenesse returned to his home in a very emotional state and told his wife:

" 'Oh, poor Proust, if only you knew. It's terrible.'

" 'What's wrong?' asked his wife.

" 'Not in front of the children, I'll tell you after our meal,' replied the physician.

"After the meal was over, the children left the table but young Chantenesse glued his ear to the dining-room door. He overheard his parents saying things about Marcel that he understood only later. His father never stopped repeating: 'Poor Adrien Proust, luckily he's got Robert.'

"It would seem that Marcel's family could not come to terms with his homosexuality," Chalon explained to me, "since they considered his brother to be the great man."

In those years, Proust complained to Bizet:

> *I've got plenty of worries, my family and I aren't getting along. I think they're going to send me away to a college in the provinces. I don't know anything about it. For how long? Maybe forever, maybe just for a couple of days. I just don't know. Why? . . . Do you think maybe it's because she finds our affection for each other a bit excessive? She's afraid it might degenerate to sensual pleasure.*

Then he declared, "I love you with all my heart."

Like Proust, Guérin also had a younger brother. Their rapport was much less strained, thanks in part to the sympathetic affinities that sometimes flourish between brothers. Both were drawn to the arts. Jacques, though a successful businessman, chemist, and manufacturer of perfumes, was an introverted bibliophile well known in Parisian cultural circles. Jean, more extroverted, was a painter, who shared many of his brother's interests. Both were sexually attracted to men. Neither hid anything from the other, but that is not to say that their relationship was uncomplicated or free of tension. Dumbfounding his older brother, Jean had let their mother know that both of her sons were homosexual. This was in 1924.

At his house on rue Berton, Guérin was still in a reverie, surrounded by the salvaged items that had come out of the hatbox. He found most remarkable a letter dated May 1888, the same year Proust had written to Bizet proclaiming his love. Guérin smiled reading these lines, written in a young person's steady hand. At the top right corner of a square yellow page he read:

Jeudi soir.

18 mai 1888

Mon cher petit grand'père

Je viens réclamer de ta gentillesse la somme
de 13 francs que je voulais demander à Monsieur
Nathan, mais que maman préfère que je te
demande. Voici pourquoi. J'avais si besoin de
voir une femme pour cesser mes mauvaises
habitudes de masturbation que papa m'a donné 10
francs pour aller au bordel. Mais 1° dans mon émotion j'ai cassé un vase de nuit, 3 francs 2° dans
cette même émotion je n'ai pas pu baiser. Me
voilà donc comme devant attendant à chaque
heure davantage 10 francs pour me vider et
en plus ces 3 francs de vase. Mais je n'ose
pas redemander sitôt de l'argent à papa et j'ai

THE LETTER TO HIS GRANDFATHER.

Thursday night

My dear grandpapa, I must ask your indulgence for the sum of 13 francs. . . . This is why. In order to desist from my nasty habit of masturbation I was so desperate to see a woman that Papa gave me 10 francs to go to a brothel. But first, in my nervous state, I broke a chamber pot, 3 francs, and then, in this same agitation, I couldn't bring myself to fuck. There I was, in for another 10 francs an hour, waiting until I could satisfy myself. . . . I wouldn't dare ask Papa for more money so soon, and I was hoping that you would help me out in this circumstance which you know is not merely exceptional, but unique: it can't happen twice in your life that you're too distraught to fuck.

Proust scholar and biographer Jean-Yves Tadié remarked upon the extreme psychological pressure and deeply inculcated morality that prompted Marcel—sent by his father, as was the custom of the period, to a brothel in order to be initiated into the mysteries of sex, and there, due to his embarrassment, breaking a chamber pot—to persist so devotedly, to try so obediently to please.

Thirty years separated Guérin from Proust, but there was a social chasm that divided them even further. As an illegitimate child, Guérin had never known conventional family life. He and his brother grew up with an unusual amount of freedom, which, among other things, had allowed them to confront their issues of sexuality more freely. That had hardly been the case for Proust, who, as German critic Walter Benjamin observed, had always remained a mama's boy. As he was to write in *Sodom and Gomorrah*, Proust believed that his sexual tastes made him a member of "a burdened, cursed race that must live by lying and perjury, all the while knowing one's desires to be criminal, disgraceful, too shameful to speak of."

Proust's homosexuality surrounded him like an invisible and insurmountable wall. His family's unwillingness to understand led to a history of silences that mutated into rancor. This in turn was transformed into acts of vandalism—papers destroyed, furniture abandoned. In the jumble of connections between son and parents, between brothers, between brother-in-law and sister-in-law, between uncle and niece, in the vicious turns of phrase referring to things said and things left unsaid, this invisible wall of Proust's homosexuality was always there, intractable.

Among the papers and photographs in the hatbox, there were also a few books, and it was here that Guérin found, to his amazement, the answer to a question he had asked Robert Proust six years earlier in his office. Guérin now held a sad, tattered book in his hands, a first edition of *Swann's Way*, printed in 1913. Inside, on an intact page that escaped Marthe's ruthless effacement of all traces of Marcel's name, Guérin discovered a dedication: *To my little brother, a souvenir of lost time, regained for a moment whenever we see one another.*

For Guérin, finding this book was a sweet reprieve; a rare volume had been spared, a victim of negligence. For all those years, Robert Proust had not remembered owning this book and had allowed time and carelessness to reduce it to a very sorry state. His memory had not retained the tender and nostalgic words of his brother's dedication, and now these words filled the room like a cry from the heart, like the pleas Proust heard from souls trapped in inanimate objects yearning to be set free.

The rapport between Marcel and Robert was always one full of affection, but it was never intimate. Love for their parents and the shared experiences of childhood united them, but they had almost nothing in common. As observed by contemporaries, however, the brothers shared several characteristics. Both were exceedingly well educated, maintained a somewhat exaggerated sense of scruples, and were inherently skeptical. Each brother also developed a remarkable capacity for understanding others. Georges Duhamel, a surgeon and writer, winner of the Prix Goncourt in 1918, remembered watching Robert Proust at work as a surgeon. He observed that his medical colleague possessed "the same slowness, the same languor, the same inclination to detour, the same paradoxical inventiveness, the same reticence. At the end of the day, Robert's surgical style had much in common with Marcel's literary phrasing."

Among the papers Werner had thrown in the hatbox was an undated letter from Marcel as a young boy to his mother, in which can be felt all the concern of an older brother for a younger sibling. In a fine, clear, almost feminine hand, Proust expressed his worry about his brother's melancholic disposition:

> *My dear Mama,*
>
> *I think Robert is feeling sad and it worries me. Not asking anything of him, I wasn't able to get a word out of him and you won't be able to do better. But he is very kind. Try and chat with him before he goes out.*

Proust always spoke of his brother's goodness, yet was invariably ironic when describing him: "Happiness and regret have ripened his nature like a fruit that, having been a trifle acidic, becomes sweet," he wrote to his mother. Followed by this: "Don't show this letter to my angel-brother because he is not only an angel but also a judge, a harsh judge." It could be that Robert was not as harsh a judge as Marcel claimed, but he certainly projected a paternalistic aura, both in his work and in his private life.

Near the end of his life, Marcel wrote to his brother asking for help in procuring the award of the Legion of Honor, through Robert's friendship with the highly influential General Charles Mangin. Robert's response was less than encouraging. Marcel wrote back to him:

Dear little brother,

Thank you with all my heart for your too kind letter. Don't worry: under no circumstances would I ever have let myself be commended by General M. By this I don't mean to say that we can act freely, and in this particular case, the only reason for the General's feelings toward me are my books. Despite this, I would never have risked upsetting your relations with him without having first received your approval. And so you tell me you would prefer that nothing be asked of him. Rest assured, your wish is an order; I will never ask anything of him. . . .

I don't spurn honorary titles, but I can live without them. The work, that's what needs to be done: whether the rest comes or doesn't is secondary.

Proust continued with a description of his ailments and with a list of physicians he was to consult. But in the last lines of his letter he exacts his small and bitter revenge:

My book, The Guermantes Way, *will be coming out the first week of October. It's only half as long as the others, but I'm sure you won't read it. . . .*

Unlike Marcel, Robert took after their father in all ways and yielded to his will: he unhesitatingly married the woman chosen for him, embraced the same medical career, had a mistress. This was a Mme Fournier, who lived in a small apartment not far from the hospital where Robert operated. On at least one occasion, during the war, Robert made his brother complicit in this arrangement, involving Marcel in a transaction to get Mme Fournier a sum of money while he was still at the front. In a letter written in 1917 to their mother's friend Mme Catusse, Marcel colors his report of this episode with an amused and smug tone:

Quite remarkably, I can give you firsthand news of Robert, who wrote to me for the first time in six months, because while he is dutiful, he is at the same time overwhelmed, by both work and laziness. He's fine. But the nature of what brought him to write to me two days ago might better remain a secret between us, and so please do not let on to my sister-in-law that I re-

ceived a letter from her husband. Since I never see Marthe, I feel no compunction to remain silent.

A complicity regarding extracurricular affairs of the heart (as common now as then, no doubt) existed between the brothers, though Proust surely knew he could never expect reciprocity on this account from Robert. He would never have dared to infringe upon the family's respectability.

Marthe certainly knew about her husband's infidelity, and she was also well aware of her brother-in-law's proclivities. During Proust's lifetime, her rapport with him was characterized by a cold politeness. When, in November 1906, Marthe's infant daughter, Suzy, contracted diphtheria, Proust wrote to his brother about his niece: "It pains me to consider this child, in whom I like to think a little bit of Mama and Papa lives on, starting life so sadly." When he telephoned Marthe to relay his concerns about Suzy's condition, she responded "with an excessive brevity," which annoyed him. "She's very nice, despite her humorlessness," he wrote to Mme Catusse about Marthe, but added, "though it is true, without realizing it, I can be disagreeable to the nth degree."

Marthe's marriage was a miserable failure: Robert had other women in his life and had managed to run through not only his considerable inheritance, but also her own sizable family resources. When Robert died, Marthe was left in serious financial straits. She nurtured a persistent indignation against the two brothers that over time festered into hate. With both brothers now dead, Marthe was determined to destroy any and all traces left of her brother-in-law: papers, books, intimate and cherished items. As for the furniture, it was as if these objects released in her resentments that had never before surfaced explicitly.

In 1906, after both parents had died, Marcel, aged thirty-five, finally moved out of his family's large rue de Courcelles apartment. Long and wearisome negotiations about the distribution of Jeanne and Adrien Proust's furniture began. The brothers exchanged letters that were cordial but not without reproach: "Keep what you want, put the rest in storage," wrote Robert, exasperated. Marcel felt that his brother's refusal to take his share of the furniture put a financial burden on him, because it meant he could not move into a smaller apartment: "You forced me into arranging my expenses, my investments, my life in a different way." As soon as Marthe took interest in a rug or a tapestry, Marcel would suddenly decide to keep it for himself.

In George Painter's biography, he commented wryly that "Proust's catalogue of furniture, in which every single object from 45 rue de Courcelles is in turn destined for every room in 102 boulevard Haussmann, or given to servants, to Robert, to Dr. Landowski, or sold, or popped into the basement, is an enormity which the biographer must spare the reader."

It was no coincidence that brother-in-law and sister-in-law harbored ambivalence and distrust for one another. Whereas Marthe consigned Marcel's desk and bookcase to a junk peddler, he had previously committed a far more sacrilegious gesture. In the spring of 1917, Albert Le Cuziat, the model for Jupien, opened a male brothel on rue de l'Arcade; the entry and single bedroom's principal furnishings included chairs, rugs, and tapestries once owned by Jeanne and Adrien Proust, a gift donated by their son. This act was transposed directly into *In Search of Lost Time*. The Narrator offers certain pieces of his aunt Léonie's furniture to the madam of a brothel:

> *But as soon as I saw them again in the house where these women were putting them to their own uses, all the virtues that I had once inhaled in my aunt's bedroom at Combray came back to me, being defenselessly tortured by the cruel contact to which I had abandoned them! Had I violated the memory of the dead, I would not have suffered such remorse. I never went back to this madam's house, because those pieces of furniture seemed to me to be alive and beckoning me, like those supposedly inanimate objects from a Persian fairy tale, in which imprisoned souls, subjected to martyrdom, implore you to free them*

This second reference to souls trapped in inanimate objects highlights Proust's fascination with the concepts of captivity and resurrection. According to the Italian scholar Mariolina Bongiovanni Bertini, the Narrator's fears come "to signify not the hope of resurrection, but rather the terror and anguish of an indefinite survival deprived of redemption."

Over a period of several months, Guérin continued to see Werner. He soon realized that the young man's relationship with Marthe was more complex than Guérin had originally imagined. Marthe clearly trusted Werner and had come to rely on him as a confidant; Guérin realized that Werner wore many hats. He would invite Werner to his house for a glass of port but then would proceed to subject him to interrogation, always wanting to know about the possibility of there being still more papers, more things. Jacques Guérin was a highly cultivated and refined man, capable of expressing extreme sensitivity and delicacy, yet he could also be mordant and caustic and act in a superior, authoritarian manner. While he may have yielded to Werner's insidious hold over him, he was never weak.

One night Werner finally gave in to Guérin's ceaseless prodding and revealed that after Marcel died, most of the vast, jumbled hoard of things that came from his rue Hamelin apartment were immediately relegated to storage in the attic of Robert Proust's avenue Hoche home. Twelve years later, when the doctor died and Marthe wanted to be rid of all of Marcel's things, she simply gave everything to Werner. He took possession of the entire inventory and removed it to his private storage space. Having known Guérin now for some time, Werner finally invited him to come and have a look, to see if there would be anything else of interest to him.

Much to his surprise, Guérin learned that Werner's stash wasn't at all far from his business, a very short drive from his factory along the river road. Up ahead, a wooden structure came into view that Guérin had driven past for years: amazingly, this was Werner's warehouse. He was incredulous when he realized that so short a distance separated his own workplace from Werner's; so short a distance between him and, as it turned out, even more of Marcel Proust's tangible remains.

At Werner's storage shed, Guérin was completely overwhelmed by what surrounded him. He found a sidewalk covered with all kinds of merchandise: mirrors, toilets, old utensils, prices scrawled in chalk. Looking carefully among all the knickknacks spread out on display, Guérin's beautiful blue eyes widened; there on the ground he saw, encased in a vulgar, ornate frame, a portrait of Dr. Adrien Proust. The broad face, with its gray beard and reproachful expression, seemed to plead with Guérin

to get him out of the mire into which he had been thrown. When speaking of this amazing find years later, Guérin recalled that it struck him as impossible that so great a humiliation could be inflicted on so distinguished a man.

Next to this painting, scattered about on the pavement, Guérin saw what he realized must have been items from Marcel Proust's toiletry set, identifying them by their engraved initials. Guérin was well aware that anyone would consider these brushes virtually worthless without the knowledge of whose hair they had combed, but knowing to whom these brushes belonged made them virtually priceless.

Guérin spotted two gilded wooden candelabra that had once pompously crowned the rosewood bookcases in the Proust family's living room on rue de Courcelles. (They can be seen in a photograph of Mme. Proust absorbed in her reading.) Underneath these, Guérin identified the rug that had once covered Proust's bedroom floor. He poked about in a box and came upon some fragile objects thrown together: a piece of jade that had been a gift from Anne de Noailles; an elegant leather case from Cartier containing a coral tie pin; and, unbelievably, the Legion of Honor medal which had once made Proust so proud. ("It's not the gift itself that so charms me, Céleste; it's the delicacy of the gesture and the thought.") Taking this small object in his hands, Guérin recalled a note from Cocteau from among the letters in the hatbox Werner had brought him, congratulating Proust for this honor: "On you the red ribbon makes sense, and I embrace you."

Guérin also spotted an elaborate pigskin cane, a gift to Proust from the Marquis d'Albufera, embellished with a gold tip on which the initials M.P. were engraved. Proust was clutching this cane in a photograph that was to become famous, one that Guérin felt was incorrectly referred to as *Proust Leaving the Jeu de Paume*. It was Guérin's belief that the photograph had been taken long before that visit to the Jeu de Paume, when Proust had experienced a distressing dizziness, which in his novel he came to attribute to Bergotte.

Guérin was overwhelmed, but also insatiable. Not satisfied with these astonishing finds, he scowled at Werner. He said he wanted to see more.

The young dealer didn't respond. Instead, he turned and went inside the shed and climbed down a stairway into the basement. Guérin followed close behind. For a collector, the latent mystery embodied in other people's belongings can ignite a covetous desire—part longing, part fulfillment—of unquantifiable value. In this particular instance, more was at stake than simple egotistical voraciousness. The thrill driving Guérin was no longer merely that of a collector, but of a savior.

Guérin followed Werner to the back of the underground space, pulled as if by a magnetic force toward some unknown revelation. What he found there, blackened and oxidized, still draped in its worn blue satin fabric, was Proust's brass bed, covered in dust. It had been his from the age of sixteen. Throughout the many years, throughout the endless nights of insomnia, Proust lay on this very bed composing his magnum opus. It was on this bed that Proust died on November 18, 1922. Walter Benjamin described this humble bed as the place where Proust "found himself torn apart by nostalgia for a changed world." In Benjamin's mind, there were only two moments in history when such a "scaffolding" was rigged up. The first was "when Michelangelo, lying prone, his head thrown back, painted the creation of the world on the Sistine ceiling." Then came "the bed on which the ailing Proust lay, pen in his raised hand, covering innumerable pages in writing consecrated to the creation of his own microcosmic world."

Guérin was so moved that tears began to well up and roll down his face. He felt that fate had rewarded him handsomely for his diligence in searching out and seeking to preserve these earthly remains of a literary deity.

The deal was quickly made. He had Werner move everything to his house on rue Berton. Guérin set aside a whole room of his house to re-create Proust's rue Hamelin bedroom, where his bed, his bookcase, his desk, and various smaller personal effects would be reunited. Looking at them all, affectionately arranged as in their previous incarnation, he felt that each of these items possessed a palpable interior life. Guérin had the impression that these objects were hovering in a space beyond time. He considered himself an agent of destiny on a mission he had never agreed to undertake; he was convinced that the impulse to preserve these precious talismans must have come from some potent force of will within him. Mysteriously, all of these objects had somehow made their way to him and he to them.

In his preface to Ruskin's *Sesame and Lilies*, Proust spoke about his bedroom:

> *I leave it to men and women of taste to furnish their rooms as a reflection of their taste, filling it only with things that suit them. For me, I can only live and think in rooms where everything is the creation, the language of lives profoundly different from mine, of a taste contrary to my own, where I find nothing of my own conscious thoughts, where my imagination is thrilled to plunge into the heart of the not-me.*

The outcome of this "agent of destiny" adventure, far from appeasing Guérin, only served to excite him more. The idea that there were still things to be reclaimed left him no peace. He was obsessed by the idea that his role as savior was not yet finished. At this point in time, according to what Guérin told Piero Tosi, he began to scour obituary listings in *Le Figaro* and to attend the funerals of Proust's friends in search of more confidences, more souvenirs.

Through it all, Guérin continued to see Werner regularly. On his way home from work, Guérin would swing by Werner's storage shed and invite him home for a drink and a bit of chat. Each time they met, he would pummel the man with refreshed vigor, always in an urgent manner, shaking him violently on occasion to get him to confess to yet one more secret sacrilege, to admit that there was still something else to be had. Guérin could lose his temper, becoming almost brutal with his incessant barrage of questions. Werner categorically denied possessing anything else but, with his instinctual sadism, let it be known that it was quite possible several things might yet have escaped Guérin's evangelical mission. This left Guérin panting for more.

Then, one evening, moving toward the door as he was about to take leave of Guérin, Werner, as if tired of concealing a minor larceny, let slip that he did have something else of Proust's that he had kept concealed from Guérin. He claimed no little embarrassment. It had to do with his love of fishing

and his ritual Sunday outings on the Marne, where he kept a small boat. Marthe, hearing about these fishing trips, told him he was crazy, that he would catch his death of cold out on the river in the middle of winter. Worried about his well-being, she presented him with an old coat of Marcel's for him to wear. Ever since, whenever he went out in his boat, he would wrap this coat around his legs and cover his feet. After all this time, Werner felt the need to unburden himself about possessing the coat and having kept it a secret from him.

Guérin was stunned. He immediately began to plead, almost hysterically, for Werner to bring him the coat, regardless of its condition or however filthy or damaged it was.

Werner, though by now long familiar with his client's peculiarities, still failed to understand the extravagance of this particular request. What possible value could there be in an old, worn-out coat, one in such a deplorable state? Such a thought made him redden with shame. He attempted to disabuse Guérin of the idea.

He was not sufficiently persuasive. In the face of

Guérin's insistence, he wound up bringing the old coat to him. He wouldn't take a cent for it.

If I try to imagine Proust, I close my eyes and see him covered in his dark coat, as he was so often described by those who knew him. Reading *In Search of Lost Time,* I can only visualize the Narrator swaddled in his otter-lined overcoat.

One night in 1901, at Chez Larue, the exclusive restaurant on place de la Madeleine, Proust complained of the cold. In quick response, Bertrand de Fénelon, one of his closest friends from among the group of young aristocrats with whom he socialized, executed the famous acrobatic stunt, which, in the novel, is attributed to Robert de Saint-Loup. From the ground, Fénelon leapt onto the back of a length of red velvet banquette in order to bring his shivering friend his heavy coat. A similar scene was repeated ten years later when, inspired by Proust's discourse in praise of the talents of Vaslav Nijinsky, premier danseur of the Ballets Russes, Jean Cocteau jumped up on the table to carry his sick friend's coat to him—an episode that would inspire Proust to write:

> Covering me in fur like a mink
> His eyes not having spilled their black ink
> Like a sylph on the ceiling, or on the snow
>   a ski
> Jean jumped on the table as if Nijinsky.

In *The Captive*, at a reception given by Mme Verdurin in honor of the violinist Morel, Baron Charlus gallantly offers to go look for the Narrator's coat, but M. Brichot responds more quickly. Brichot returns, mistakenly having retrieved the Baron's coat instead of the Narrator's. The Baron is indignant: "But what's this? That's my coat he's carrying. I would have been better off going myself." Turning to the Narrator, he affectionately says: "Here, put this on your shoulders." Then, "Do you realize this puts you in a very compromising position, *mon cher*? It's as if we were both drinking out of the same glass; I'll be able to read your thoughts."

From the time he was a child, Proust dressed with

extreme care, but in a very peculiar fashion. According to Léon Pierre-Quint, an early biographer, young Proust "looked like a cross between a refined dandy and an untidy medieval philosopher. He wore poorly knotted cravats under a turned-down collar, or large silk shirtfronts from Charvet in a creamy pink whose exact tint he spent a long time tracking down. He was slender enough to indulge in a double-breasted waistcoat, and sported a rose or an orchid in the buttonhole of his frock coat. He wore very light-colored gloves with black points, which were often soiled and crumpled; these he bought at Trois Quartiers because Robert de Montesquiou bought his there. A flat-brimmed top hat and a cane completed the elegant look of this slightly disheveled Beau Brummell. Even on the hottest days of summer he had on a heavy fur-lined coat, which became legendary among those who knew him."

From the age of twenty, Proust dressed in this fashion. He never changed his look, which gave people the impression that time had stood still for him. It was as if he had been embalmed in his youth. For those who saw him for the first time, the effect was like coming upon an apparition. In his memoir, *The Night Visitor,* Proust's friend Paul Morand described him as "a very pale man, encased in an old fur-lined coat; thick black hair cut at the nape of his neck, in the style of 1905, sticking out from under his gray bowler hat; his hands in slate-colored kid gloves holding on to a cane: a soft shadow of blue across the bottom of his dull ivory cheeks; his teeth were large and shiny; his mustache accentuated his heavy eyebrows; a velvety, deep regard emanated from darkened eyelids, which veiled his magnetism."

Thus Proust sauntered among the sumptuous rooms of the Ritz. He would travel down the long corridor of the renowned hotel on place Vendôme, making his way to the restaurant, walking with a sort of unsteady slowness. As he entered, always perfectly aware of the stares focused on him, he was gawked at by the other diners. In a letter, Sir Philip Sassoon, the grandson of Baron Gustave de Rothschild, told an anecdote about Proust with characteristic sarcasm: "One of your most illustrious compatriots pleased me by saying, 'The biggest thrill my wife and I brought home with us from Paris was seeing Monsieur Proust.' I was very impressed, until he added, 'He was the first man we've ever seen eating in a fur coat.' "

As the critic Edmond Jaloux remembered, Proust didn't walk, he just "appeared." And at the height of spring, he would "appear," still enveloped in his heavy overcoat, like "a shadow born from his smoky fumigations, his face and voice devoured by his nocturnal habits," as Paul Morand wrote in his "Ode to Marcel Proust." He would sit down at a table and order very little to eat or drink, although one night he did put away an entire bottle of Porto 345. This particular brand is then cited in the novel by M. de Cambremer, who, while chatting with Dr. Cottard at the Verdurins, praises the port's ability to combat insomnia.

In 1913, Cocteau penned a written portrait of Proust, portraying him as he "returned at dawn from his nightly drives, huddled in his fur-lined overcoat, deathly pale, his eyes dark as coal, a liter of Evian water jutting out of his pocket." To accompany this description, Cocteau drew a sketch of his subject, wrapped in his bulky overcoat, his chin buried in its fur collar, his mustache as black as the hair sticking out from under his hat. Several

COCTEAU'S DRAWING.

smudged pencil strokes represent his darkened eyes and his badly shaved cheeks.

Guérin owned this drawing; it was part of the treasure from the hatbox. He framed it in a dark mat, heightening the contrast between the pale yellow sheet and the dark lines Cocteau had drawn. Guérin had had this done long before he learned that the overcoat in the sketch was still being used to protect a peddler's legs from a river's winter cold.

Finally Guérin came to own the coat, the ultimate relic, so evocative of the physical form of the writer. "I can still see his appalling bedroom on the rue Hamelin," the Nobel laureate François Mauriac recounted of his meeting with Proust on February 28, 1921, "the blackened hearth, the bed where his overcoat served as a blanket, the waxen mask from behind which one could say our host watched us eat. His hair seemed to be the only thing that was alive." The overcoat was ever-present.

Sometimes Guérin would delicately fondle his prized possession, fingering the buttons that had been altered to fit Werner's younger and smaller body. He would stroke the discolored fur collar that had been ravaged by the water of the Marne. Rubbing this tattered material between his fingers he felt the same emotion as when he was rifling through the pages of a rare book once believed to be lost. Something that needed to be saved had found its way to him.

Guérin had the overcoat cleaned, had it smartened up, and ordered a teak box to preserve it from the ravages of time. On the outside of the box his old housekeeper lettered the words: PROUST'S OVERCOAT.

The knack Guérin had for discovering and marketing new, enormously commercial perfumes continued to make him rich, and over the years he came to be known not only as a bibliophile but also as a patron of the arts. His "nose" led him to nurture the new talents he came across in the artistic and literary salons of Paris; he was always stimulated by the prospect of protecting something rare and precious. From Maurice Sachs, a novelist and shady character associated with many Parisian writers, Guérin bought the autograph manuscripts of Raymond Radiguet's novels that Cocteau had sold to finance his opium habit; he then donated them to the Bibliothèque Nationale. His was an insatiable appetite, a sort of carnal love for unique objects. Guérin must have relished this description of longing in *Sodom and Gomorrah*, of a man's craving for a woman he has dreamed about, who he knows need not be beautiful to be desirable:

> *These desires are only the desire for this or that person; vague as perfumes, as styrax was the desire of Prothyraïa, saffron the ethereal desire, spices the desire of Hera, myrrh the perfume of the clouds, manna the desire of Nike, incense the perfume of the sea. But these perfumes that are sung in the Orphic hymns are far fewer in number than the deities they cherish. Myrrh is the perfume of the clouds, but also of Protogonos, of Neptune, of Nereus, of Leto; incense is the perfume of the sea, but also of the fair Dike, of Themis, of Circe, of the nine Muses, of Eos, of Mnemosyne, of the Day, of Dikaïosyne. As for styrax, manna and spices, it would be impossible to name all the deities that inspire them, so many are they. Amphietes has all the perfumes except incense, and Gaïa rejects only beans and spices. So it was with these desires that I felt for different girls. Less numerous than the girls themselves, they changed into disappointments and regrets closely similar one to another. I never wished for myrrh. I reserved it for Jupien and for the Princesse*

de Guermantes, for it is the desire of Protogonos "of the two sexes, with that roar of a bull, of countless orgies, memorable, descending joyously to the sacrifices of the Orgiophants."

How this language must have been familiar to the perfume maker Guérin!

He began to spend his summers near Chantilly, in the Val d'Oise, just north of Paris. Guérin bought a house designed at the end of the eighteenth century by the neoclassical architect François-Joseph Bélanger, for his mistress, the soprano Sophie Arnould. Here he was able to provide a home for Jean Genet upon his release from prison; here he nurtured and encouraged the writer. In 1947, Guérin created a perfume he called Divine, inspired by the transvestite character in Genet's *Our Lady of the Flowers*. The novelist reciprocated the compliment in his own way, dedicating his next novel, *Querelle de Brest*, to Guérin, with words that reveal the depth of Genet's understanding of his benefactor: "There is no better way to express my gratitude than by proclaiming the joy I feel in knowing a reader for whom fetishism is a religion."

Genet introduced his patron to Violette Leduc,

who, thanks to Guérin, was able to have a deluxe edition of her autobiographical novel, *L'Affamée*, published. This she dedicated to Guérin, as she did her novel *Thérèse et Isabelle*, initially rejected by publishers in 1955 for its scandalous lesbian sex scenes, but which finally appeared to much acclaim in 1966.

Years went by, and with the passage of time, Guérin began to enter into Marthe's good graces, helping her financially through the purchase of manuscripts still in her possession. An almost affectionate relationship developed between them.

Marthe must have been enraged and wounded by the knowledge of the relationship between Dr. Adrien Proust and her mother. That affair had led directly to her own marriage to Robert Proust, who, like his father, had also come to keep a mistress. If she had taken the time to read some of Marcel's books before having spurned them, Marthe might have found the passage in the novel where the Narrator addresses Dr. Cottard's infidelity, revealed to his wife only after his death. Mme Cottard discovered correspondence that exposed her husband's long-standing liaison with Odette de Crécy. The Narrator tried his best to console Mme Cottard, explaining to her that "from the moment he was unfaithful to you, he took great care that you would never know, he worried about hurting you, he respected you and always preferred you. . . . In heaven it is you alone that he longs to see again." Proust undoubtedly wrote these lines thinking about his mother, but with neither the culture nor the refinement of his mother, his sister-in-law might still have found comfort in them.

Marthe was beset by familial grief and dire economic straits. She never understood, she could never fathom, the elevated stature held by her brother-in-law in the world of letters. She could not bring herself to read *In Search of Lost Time.* What mattered to her was to remove all trace of indecency liable to expose the family name to shame and disgrace.

In this spirit of vengeance, Marcel Proust's love letters were destroyed, as well as reams of his worldly correspondence, and most egregiously, innumerable drafts and working notes for his great masterwork. In the nick of time, Guérin had appeared and managed to save many priceless treasures, including the thirteen notebooks Robert Proust never surrendered to Marcel's publishers, once feared missing.

These books contained variations of the final sections of *In Search of Lost Time*, which Proust wrote and rewrote more than ten times. (When Guérin ultimately sold these notebooks to the Bibliothèque Nationale, a definitive edition of the novel was finally realized, the myriad variations appearing in voluminous appendices.) Many letters were saved from destruction, but also the first edition of *Swann's Way*, published in 1913 by Grasset, corrected in Proust's hand, which Christie's sold for a dizzying sum in London on June 7, 2000.

The feelings of disdain Guérin used to harbor for Marthe gradually subdued over time. Reassured of her good faith, he began to pay social calls on her. The workings of her heart remained impenetrable, but ultimately a certain trust was established between them. Guérin, habitually curious, learned that Marthe's daughter was the primary focus of her anxiety. Marthe confessed to him that she found Suzy cold and unforgiving with her. That the young woman was venal and self-absorbed was only too clear to Guérin.

Economic difficulties forced Marthe to sell her house. She had to content herself with renting part of a large apartment whose entrance had to be shared with the proprietor. She asked Guérin how he thought she could manage this when people came to visit. He proposed that she post the name Proust on the door next to the names of the other people in the house. Marthe became indignant and exclaimed: "I'll never use that name again."

Guérin continued to visit her even when she was quite old, providing her with a little company. One evening, after restating his belief in her brother-in-law's genius, he screwed up his courage and asked her directly why she had never read his book. In the dry-toned voice of a well-brought-up woman of the bourgeoisie who knew her place, she calmly stated that she knew what he wrote was only lies.

Philip Kolb, the man who devoted a large part of his life to bringing coherence to the infinite mass of Marcel's correspondence, fared no better. To the insistent questions put to her, Marthe gave him equally acerbic responses. Regarding the anecdotes, the details, but especially her personal memories of Proust, Marthe, irritated, offered the American specialist this lapidary judgment: "*Monsieur*, my brother-in-law was one very bizarre person."

Not another word.

"The tombs in the Père Lachaise cemetery are open books that reveal their verdicts," Giuseppe Marcenaro wrote in his book *Cemeteries.*

In the northwest section of Père Lachaise cemetery, beneath the bare slab of dark marble where Marcel rests along with his father, Adrien; his mother, Jeanne; and his brother, Robert; Marthe Dubois-Amiot also lies. Never would she have thought of sharing her eternal repose with the Proust family.

Many years later, in the 1960s, Guérin continued to make the trip between his house in the Val d'Oise and the factory of Parfums d'Orsay in Puteaux. His life went on as usual, and the years brought him new friends and new adventures. One day, while out riding in his car near Chantilly, he noticed a new antiques store by the side of the road. Curious as ever, he pulled over, parked his car, and went inside. Behind a table laden with goods, he spotted the engaging smile of the solicitous owner. Thirty years had passed but he knew right away it was Werner. They embraced like old compatriots who find each other again after many years. They sat and talked and caught up with the same enthusiasm they had long before; naturally the subject of Proust's overcoat came up.

In Werner's company, Guérin had the feeling that time had not moved; his memories had such freshness about them. He began to speak to Werner about his current high esteem for Marthe, and, quite moved, referred to the sad life to which she had been reduced.

Werner would have none of it, rejecting outright the notion of Marthe's sad life. A large smile lit up his face. (Guérin was once again reminded of the boys of Pigalle.) He asked Guérin to consider why it was that Marthe had been so considerate to him, a humble peddler; why it might have been that she decided to bestow her brother-in-law's fur-lined coat upon him, to keep him warm while out on the river. If you only knew, he said to Guérin, what went on between Marthe and me. . .

The eloquence of the gesture he made while speaking revealed more than any words could have. Guérin, a man who relished hidden things, was totally dumbstruck by this revelation of passions long concealed.

In later years, when he would tell the story of the

BIBLIOTHÈQUE JACQUES GUÉRIN

SEPTIÈME PARTIE

LIVRES

ET

MANUSCRITS

IMPORTANTS

PARIS

20 MAI 1992

GUÉRIN LIBRARY SALE CATALOG.

overcoat to his friends, Guérin would wryly add that he had told them Werner had worn many hats.

Jacques Guérin was ninety-eight when he died in August 2000. He had amassed one of the most important personal libraries of his time. He had been slavishly attached to his hard-won trophies, the papers he guarded tenaciously, the delicate objects he cherished (as Genet noted) to the point of fetishism, the mementos of both well-known and unknown personalities he loved with an almost maniacal obsession. He was proud of the souvenirs that came to him as a result of his willingness to get involved, as in the case of Proust, with friends and family, in the hopes of acquiring one more keepsake, one more palpable testimony.

Guérin lived like a Renaissance prince in his castle packed with treasures. In vain, the president of the French Republic, François Mitterrand, twice paid him a visit in the hopes of acquiring the priceless collection for the Bibliothèque Nationale. According to Carlo Jansiti, who was present,

Guérin treated Mitterrand much as he did everyone else: with great courtesy, warmth, and wonderful conversation. He put on a splendid breakfast for his honorable guest. But the script was always the same. When guests hinted at the real purpose of their visit, Guérin would politely interrupt and pretend surprise: "What a shame! We talked so much and it's getting to be evening. So it's too late now to show you . . . or discuss. . . . Maybe another time." Invariably they were bitterly disappointed; many were annoyed. One after another they would be accompanied quietly to their cars by Guérin, who then returned to his revered solitude.

For more than fifty years he had kept his secret cache tucked away. Turning ninety, he decided the time had come to sell his extraordinary collection, to separate himself from his things. In so doing, he came to acknowledge that everything passes, everything disappears. He had sought out his treasures passionately, had loved them, but he had never exhibited them, preferring instead to preserve them exclusively for his own pleasure. "When a man loves a woman, he doesn't share her with others," he confided to the poet Franco Marcoaldi in an interview. "I was like that with my treasures. Like Bluebeard with his women, I kept them in my closet."

At three o'clock one May afternoon in 1992, at the Hôtel George V in Paris, a public auction of Guérin's prized collection of manuscripts and first editions was held. Included were books and papers by writers and artists such as Apollinaire, Baudelaire, Cocteau, Genet, Hugo, Picasso, Rimbaud, and of course Proust. Letters, drafts, and photographs, some of which had come out of the enchanted hatbox in the house on rue Berton, were sold for staggering amounts of money.

To those, like me, who had not known him, Jacques Guérin was an indecipherable spirit. On the threshold of a new century, all passion spent, he was finally able to serenely separate himself from his beloved holdings. He confided to Marcoaldi, "My collection is like an air balloon. The years pass and I rise up heavenward."

MUSÉE CARNAVALET.

Conclusion

Unknown to us are the names of the buyers who paid exorbitant sums at auction for Proust's letters, drafts, sketches, and notebooks from Guérin's collection. These collectors undoubtedly guard the treasures now in their possession with jealousy and fervor equal to Guérin's.

But if you happen to be in Paris and feel like taking a stroll through the Musée Carnavalet, be sure to climb what long ago was Mme de Sévigné's magnificent stairway. One floor up, you'll find rooms devoted to Paris at the dawn of the twentieth century; having made your way through several of these, you will come to a narrow hallway. Look to your right and you'll see Mme de Noailles's luminous, ultra-feminine bedroom, with its elegant Louis XVI bed. The next room you come to is cordoned off by a length of chain. A notice informs you that the furnishings on display came from Marcel Proust's bedroom, a gift to the museum from M. Jacques Guérin. The museum guidebook will tell you that "the furniture and objects assembled here accompanied Marcel Proust to the three dwellings he occupied after the death of his parents, from the moment when, after a frivolous youth, he withdrew bit by bit from the world to consecrate his energies almost exclusively to his writing. Being in the habit of writing at night while in bed, it was in this modest brass bed that he composed the majority of *In Search of Lost Time*, a principal milestone of world literature."

Here you will find several of the key players from this story, carefully arranged as Proust would have seen them upon waking from sleep in his rue Hamelin apartment: the brass bed covered with a blue satin counterpane, the black bookcase and black desk, the gilded wood candelabra, the severe portrait of Dr. Adrien Proust seated on a neo-Renaissance armchair.

Spread out on a little table, various small precious objects are presented, including the Legion of Honor medal, the Cartier tie pin, and at the foot of the bed, Proust's pigskin cane. On the floor you will see the old rug that Guérin had come across at Werner's shed, caked in dirt.

Standing before this fairly conventional furniture, one might well wonder why an extremely cultivated and refined man would consider devoting considerable time, resources, energy, and passion to keeping these humble objects from neglect or even destruction. One answer could be found within the first pages of *In Search of Lost Time*:

> *Perhaps the immobility of the things around us is imposed on them by our certainty that they are themselves and not anything else, by the immobility of our thought concerning them. So it always happened that when I awoke like this, and my mind struggled unsuccessfully to discover where I was, everything revolved around me in the darkness, things, countries, years. . . . These revolving and confused evocations never lasted for more than a few seconds; often, in my*

brief uncertainty as to where I was, I did not distinguish the various suppositions of which it was composed any better than when, watching a horse run, we isolate the successive positions of its body when shown on a kinetoscope. But I saw again now one, now another of the rooms I had inhabited during my life, and in the end I would recall them all in the long reveries that followed my waking. . . . Habit! That skillful but slow-moving arranger who begins by letting our minds suffer for weeks on end in temporary quarters, but whom our minds are nonetheless only too happy to discover at last, for without it, reduced to their own devices, they would be powerless to make any room seem habitable.

Certainly I was now well awake; my body had veered around for the last time and the good angel of certainty had made all the surrounding objects stand still, had set me down under my bedclothes, in my bedroom, and had fixed, approximately in their right places in the uncertain light, my chest of drawers, my writing table, my fireplace, the window overlooking the street, and both the doors.

If it were possible for visitors to get close to the brass bed and run their hands over the faded blue counterpane, they might be surprised to find a small rectangle of the material missing. Jacques

Guérin cut off this small strip of fabric right before the bed was packed up and moved from his house to the museum. The critic and novelist René de Ceccatty saw this cutting framed and mounted beside Guérin's bed, hung like a relic, like a miraculous remnant from a medieval saint's vestment.

The overcoat is not there to be seen on exhibit in the room at the Musée Carnavalet. A small notice by the side of an armchair, given by the family of Reynaldo Hahn, states that the fragile condition of the coat prevents it from remaining on display.

Proust's overcoat is wrapped between sheets of tissue paper at the bottom of a large cardboard box on the top shelf of the museum's storeroom.

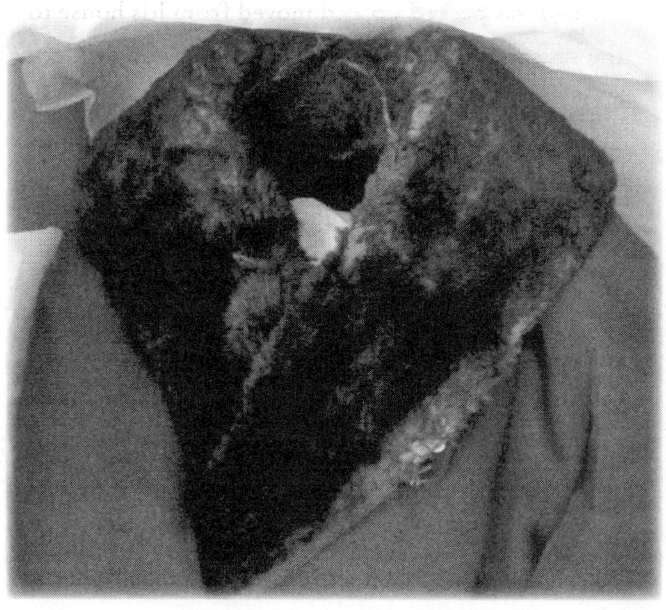

LORENZA AND LERI WITH COAT.

Acknowledgments

I wish to thank warmly the great costume designer Piero Tosi, who introduced me to this wonderful story. I also thank Carlo Jansiti, who was very close to Jacques Guérin, for furnishing me with indispensable details for the reconstruction of this story. I equally wish to acknowledge Jean-Marc Léri, director of the Musée Carnavalet, who allowed me to see the overcoat of Proust several times; Silvio Levi, president of Calé Perfumes, who gave me the chance to understand Guérin's professional activities better; Giuseppe Girimonti Greco, for his linguistic consultation; and Valeria Dani.

I offer a special thank-you to Andrea Carandini who, in friendship, but especially with the patience of an archaeologist, minutely ransacked this book and lavishly offered his precious advice.

Acknowledgments

Special praise to Portaparole, which originally published the book in Italian and in French.

Many thanks to Benedetta Craveri, the author of such unforgettable books about France. She has been so generous and encouraging to me.

I would also like to thank my agent, Ellen Levine; my publisher, Daniel Halpern; and my editor, Abigail Holstein, for their marvelous work.

Bibliography

Albaret, Celeste. *Monsieur Proust*. Paris: Laffont, 1973. (*Monsieur Proust*, trans. Barbara Bray. New York: New York Review Books Classics, 2003.)

Beauvais, Marie-Odile. *Proust vous écrira*. Paris: Melville, 2004.

Benjamin, Walter. *Oeuvres*. Vol. 2. Paris: Gallimard, 2005. (*Illuminations*. New York: Schocken, 1969.)

Bibesco, Marthe. *Al ballo con Marcel Proust*. Palermo: Sellerio, 1978.

Bloch-Dano, Evelyne. *Madame Proust*. Paris: Grasset, 2005.

Bongiovanni Bertini, Mariolina. Introduction to *Marcel Proust Scritt mondani e letterari*.Turin: Einaudi, 1984.

Cabre, Monique. *La légende du chevalier d'Orsay/Parfums de dandy*. Toulouse: Editions Milan, 1997.

Chalon, Jean. *Journal de Paris*. Paris: Plon, 2000.

Cocteau, Jean. *Journal d'un inconnu*. Paris: Grasset, 1959.

———. *Opium*. Paris: Stock, 1930.

———. *La difficulté d'être*. Paris: Morihien, 1947.

Galateria, Daria. Introduction to *Ritorno a Guermantes*. Pordenone: Studio Tesi, 1988.

Jaloux, Edmond. *Avec Marcel Proust*. Geneva: Palatine, 1953.

Jansiti, Carlo. "Violette Leduc et Jacques Guérin" in *L'amour fou*. Paris: Maren Sell, 2006.

———. *Violette Leduc*. Paris: Grasset, 1999.

———. "Le roman balzacien des souvenirs de Proust." *Le Figaro Litteraire*, March 14, 1988.

Leduc, Violette. *L'Affamée*. Paris: Gallimard, 1948.

———. *La folie en tête*. Paris: Gallimard, 1994.

———. *Correspondence*. Edited by Carlo Jansiti. Paris: Gallimard, 2007.

Liaut, Jean-Noel. *Madeleine Castaing*. Paris: Payot, 2008.

Marcenaro, Giuseppe. *Cimiteri—Storie di rimpianti e di follie*. Milan: Bruno Mondadori, 2008.

Marcoaldi, Franco. "Proust va al bordello." *La Repubblica*, April 2, 1992.

Mauriac, François. *Du côté de chez Proust*. Paris: La Table Ronde, 1947.

Mauriac-Dyer, Nathalie. *Robert Proust et la Nouvelle Revue Française*. Les Cahiers de la NFR. Paris: Gallimard, 1999.

Morand, Paul. *Tendres stocks*. Paris: Gallimard, 1921.

———. *Le visiteur du soir*. Geneva: Palatine, 1949.

Painter, George D. *Marcel Proust*. Milan: Feltrinelli, 1970. (*Marcel Proust: A Biography*, 2 vols. New York: Random House, 1959.)

Pechenard, Christian. *Proust et son père*. Paris: Quai Voltaire, 1993.

Pierre-Quint, Leon. *Marcel Proust, sa vie, son oeuvre*. Paris: Editions du Sagittaire, 1925. (*Marcel Proust: His Life and Work,* trans. Hamish Miles and Sheila Miles. New York: Knopf, 1927.)

Satie, Erik. *Correspondence presque complète*. Edited by Ornella Volta. Paris: Fayard, 2000.

Soupault, Robert. *Marcel Proust du côté de la médecine*. Paris: Plon,1967.

Tadié, Jean-Yves. *Proust*. Paris: Gallimard, 1999. (Translated by Evan Cameron as *Marcel Proust: A Life.* New York: Viking, 2000.)

———. *Proust/L'opera, la vita, la critica*. Milan: Net Il Saggiatore, 2000.

Thomson, Valentine. "My Cousin Marcel Proust." *Harper's Magazine*, May 1932.

White, Edmund. *Genet: A Biography.* New York: Alfred A. Knopf, 1993.

———. *My Lives*. New York: Ecco, 2006.

MARCEL PROUST

A la recherche du temps perdu. 4 vols. Edited by Jean-Yves Tadié. Bibliothèque de la Pléiade. Paris: Gallimard, 1987–89.

Bibliography

Alla ricerca del tempo perduto. Translated by Giovanni Raboni, annotated by Alberto Beretta Anguissola and Daria Galateria. Milan: Mondadori, 1986.

Correspondance de Marcel Proust. 20 vols. Edited by Philip Kolb. Paris: Plon,1970–92.

In Search of Lost Time. Translated by C. K. Scott Moncrieff and Terence Kilmartin. Revised by D. J. Enright. New York: Modern Library, 2003.

Lettres (1879–1922). Preface by Katherine Kolb. Paris: Plon, 2004.

Poesie. Translated by Franco Fortini. Turin: Einaudi, 1983.

Preface to *Sesamo e i gigli* by John Ruskin. Milan: Editoriale Nuova, 1982.

Bibliothèque Jacques Guérin / Livres et manuscrits importants. Catalog from the auction held at Hôtel George V, Paris, by J. Tajan, May 20, 1992.